NATIONAL GEOGRAPHIC

Ladder

TRANSFORMERS

GENRE Social Studies Article

Read to find out what makes Gee's Bend quilts special.

THE QUILTERS OF

Think about all the things that you throw away. What other uses could the objects have, outside of the purpose for which they were made? Can objects or materials have a new purpose? In other words, can they be **"repurposed"**? When we make something new with something old, we are not only being thrifty or saving money, we are using our imaginations to think differently about how we use things and how we might reuse them.

Do you ever wonder what happens to your old clothing? Maybe you cut up the clothes for rags, or maybe you donate the clothes when you outgrow them. In Gee's Bend, a small, quiet town in Alabama, several generations of women have been using old clothes and cloth scraps to create amazing quilts. Alone, clothing scraps cannot do much good, but pieced together,the scraps become quilts with vibrant colors and lively patterns. These quilts are not only beautiful to look at, but they also provide warmth in colder seasons.

GEE'S BEND

by Brigetta Christensen

Why is the work of these women notable? What makes the quilts of Gee's Bend special and sought after? It's likely that outsiders who visited Gee's Bend saw the **artistry** in the quilters' work. It was clear that the **transformation** of old scraps of cloth to beautifully designed and useful art in the form of quilts was an unusual feat.

NECESSITY DRIVES INVENTION

The tradition of quilting in Gee's Bend, Alabama, began at the turn of the 20th century. Gee's Bend is nestled within the U-shaped portion of the Alabama River. Many residents were descendants of slaves and lived very simply. One woman in the Gee's Bend quilting community remembers looking for paper to feed the old heater. Homes in this southern area weren't designed with heating systems like homes in the northern United States. Yet even though Gee's Bend is in the south, temperatures still become chilly. Folks used newspapers to plaster the walls of their drafty houses. The men and women worked long hours on their farms. They quickly and easily wore through their rugged denim and wool work clothes.

Families did not have the money to buy blankets to keep warm, and discarding perfectly good material was unthinkable. So quilters used whatever scraps of cloth that were on hand: strips of denim or pants legs, corduroy, and other inexpensive cloth to make quilts to keep their families warm.

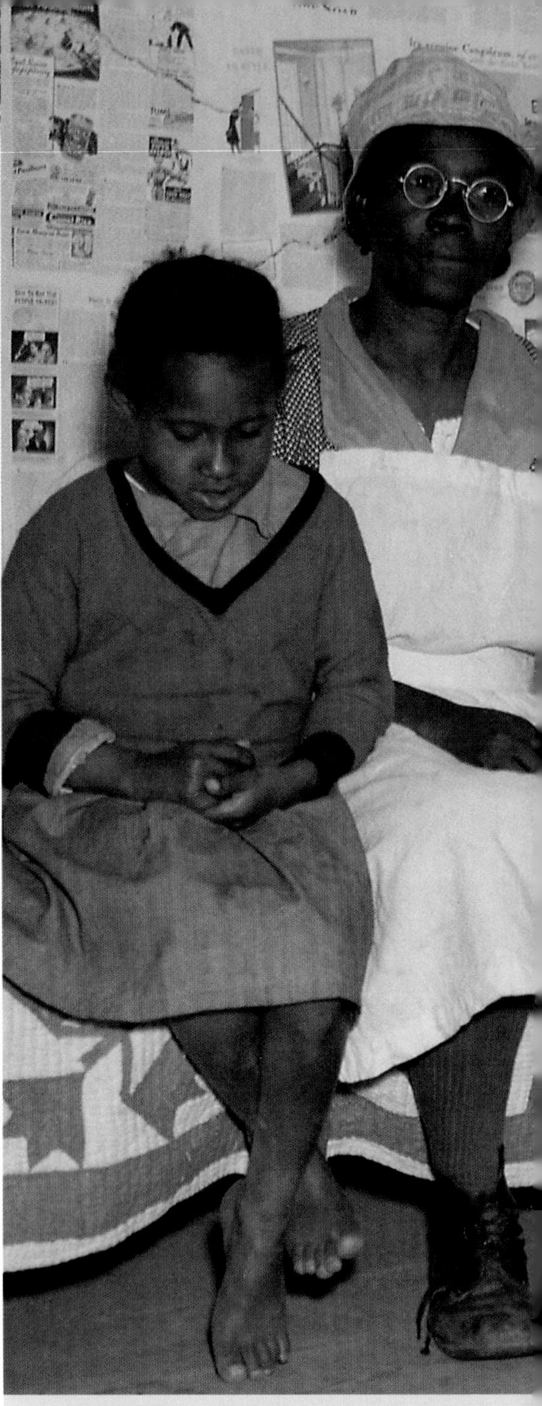

THE CRAFT OF

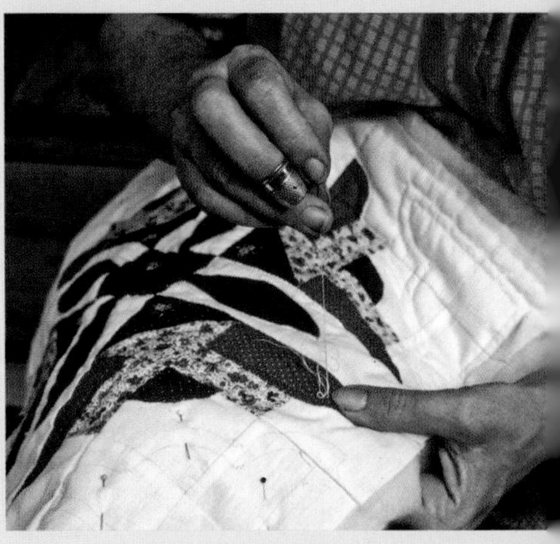

The collage effect of the newspaper wall covering inspired certain quilt patterns.

QUILTING

All quilts require the same layers to be true quilts. Quilts have a top layer of pieces. They have a middle layer of batting. And the back layer is called backing. Putting all three layers together is called basting. Sometimes a form is used to hold the three layers in place as the quilt is basted. Other times, quilters baste the layers together free-hand. Quilters use lots of pins to secure the pieces.

A pincushion secures pins and loose bits of thread.

Today, the stitching is most often done on a sewing machine. In the past, many quilters sewed each piece of the top layer by hand, only using a needle and thread.

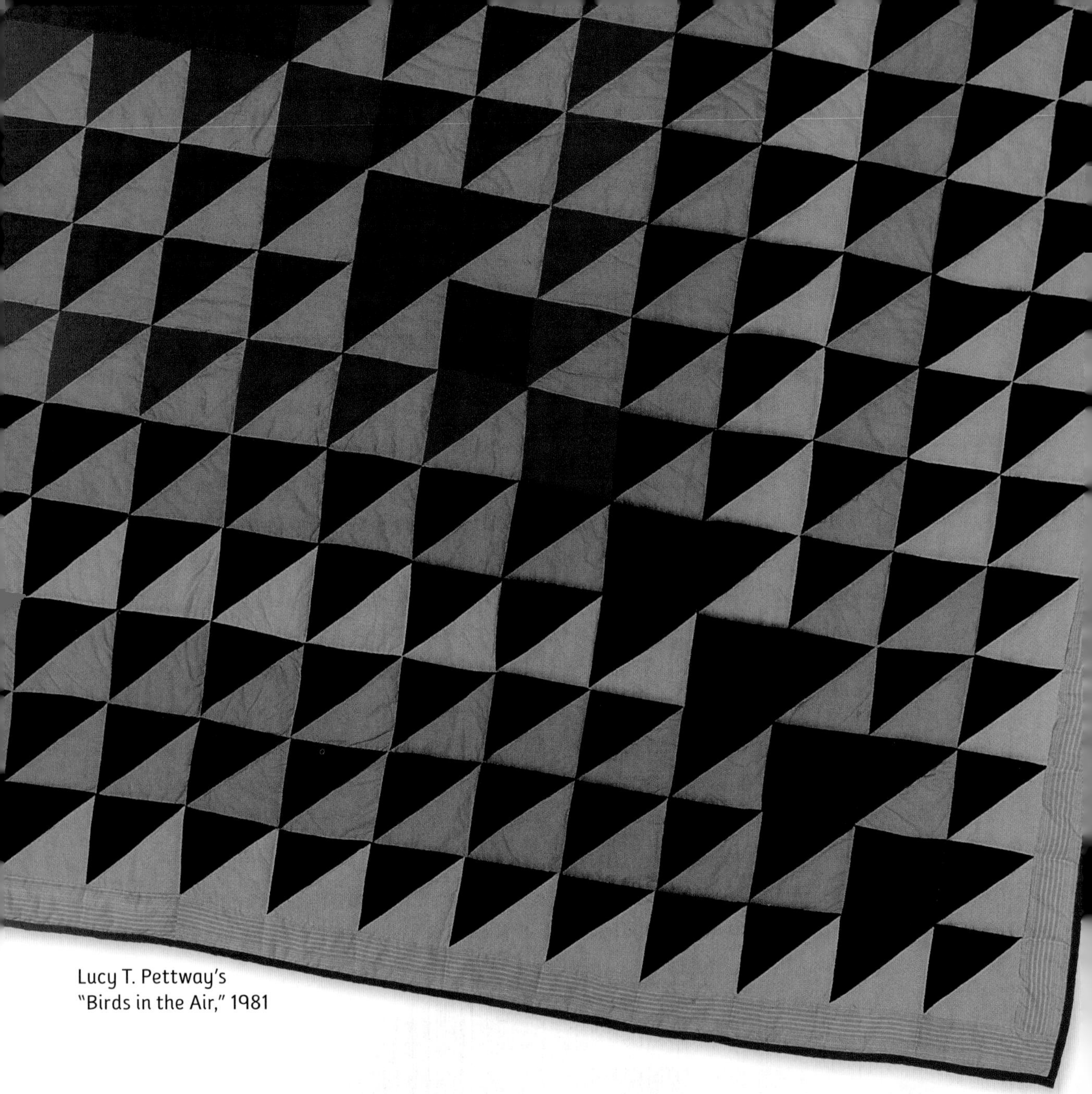

Lucy T. Pettway's
"Birds in the Air," 1981

TRANSFORMING TRADITION

In 1966, combining skill with hopes of economic advancement, quilters in Gee's Bend formed a quilting collective, or cooperative group, known as the Freedom Quilting Bee. Their work helped earn money for basics their families needed, but it also established a place to practice their craft while designing patterns completely unique to the quilter.

The quilt collective was a transformation, in that what was once an individual endeavor became a group effort. The technique of quilting also underwent a transformation. Young quilters were encouraged by their elders to follow their instincts and create their own patterns rather than anyone else's patterns.

corduroy and cotton quilt by
China Pettway, circa 1975

Arcola Pettway's "Lazy Gal," 1976

cotton quilt by Jessie T. Pettway, 1950s

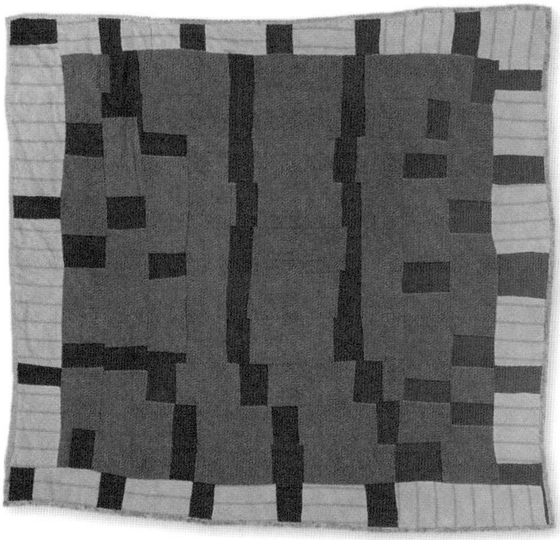

Missouri Pettway's
"Path through the Woods," 1971

Most quilters learned at their mothers' sides when they were girls. Gee's Bend has at least six generations of quilters following the traditions established by the earliest members of the Gee's Bend community. Members of the Pettway family made many of the quilts in the Quilts of Gee's Bend™ collection. Each relative used what she learned from older family members to create her own designs. Many other families in the area can boast of several generations of quilters—mothers, daughters, aunts, cousins—all contributing to this quilting tradition.

ART OR CRAFT?

In Gee's Bend, women created quilts for practical reasons. Yet the quilters experienced the creative process in much the same way as painters, sculptors, and designers. However, the creative work and the practical purpose for the quilts were equally important. For this reason, and possibly because of modesty, or not wanting to praise themselves, the quilters of Gee's Bend didn't consider their work at the level of artwork found in museums. But art critics did.

Art critics saw the same quality of artistry and invention in the Gee's Bend quilts as in the work of celebrated artists of mid-20th century art. The width and length of a quilted blanket is like the surface of a canvas used for paint. When making this comparison, the shapes, the placement of colors, and the intentional imperfections seem like a modern art painting.

Once the art world discovered the amazing quilts of Gee's Bend, they became examples of mid-20th century art, too. Certain quilt patterns have been compared to designs of artists like Mark Rothko and Paul Klee. The quilts seem to fit right in with the abstract style of modern art celebrated in galleries. And in 2002, the Houston Museum of Fine Arts presented the first exhibit of 70 quilts from Gee's Bend. The initial exhibit traveled to cities across the United States. And in 2003, all the living quilters of Gee's Bend formed a new group, The Gee's Bend Quilters Collective. The Collective is owned and operated by the quilters who continue to make original masterpieces.

No. 5/No. 22. 1950 (dated on reverse 1949). Oil on canvas, 9' 9" x 8' 11 1/8" (297 x 272 cm). Gift of the artist.

A museum curator walks through the Gee's Bend quilt exhibit. This photo shows the exhibit at the High Museum of Art in Atlanta in 2006.

These works by Mark Rothko (left) and Paul Klee (right) show bold colors. Both artists were very important in modern art movements such as abstract expressionism.

Mountain Village (Autumnal) 1934, (no 209). Oil on primed canvas on wooden panel, 2' 4 1/8" x 1' 9 1/2" (71.5 x 54.4 cm).

Nettie Young's
"Milky Way," 1971

DOING IT YOURSELF

Originally out of a need to reuse and repurpose the only materials available, the women of Gee's Bend passed down the legacy of quilt making. Many mothers told their daughters that they'd have to make what they wanted to have: dresses, quilts, and all other things for their home. But each member of this community also learned that in making something yourself, you can find a form of self-expression.

The practice of making objects by hand is a part of many eras and cultures. Throughout history, people have encountered times when buying new items wasn't economically realistic. People also discovered that making something yourself is pleasurable. It's fun to see what can result from simple materials and a little time and patience.

Jorena Pettway and her daughter sew on their front porch, 1939.

Whether out of **necessity** or respect for handmade, self-crafted products, people today are returning to the crafting traditions. People are cooking, sewing, and knitting clothes. They are building tables and cabinets. And yes, they are quilting. This trend is called DIY (Do-It-Yourself). Some DIYers turn to relatives and friends for instruction, but for many others the Internet has helped preserve and pass along traditions. For years and years, people bought clothes, blankets, toys, and furniture made elsewhere and with little understanding of what went into making these items. Now people are learning how to do-it-themselves. The women of Gee's Bend model how it's possible to make something beautiful from the simplest of materials.

Check In How did the quilters transform fabric scraps?

GENRE How-to Article

Read to find out how to make an inexpensive, handmade toy.

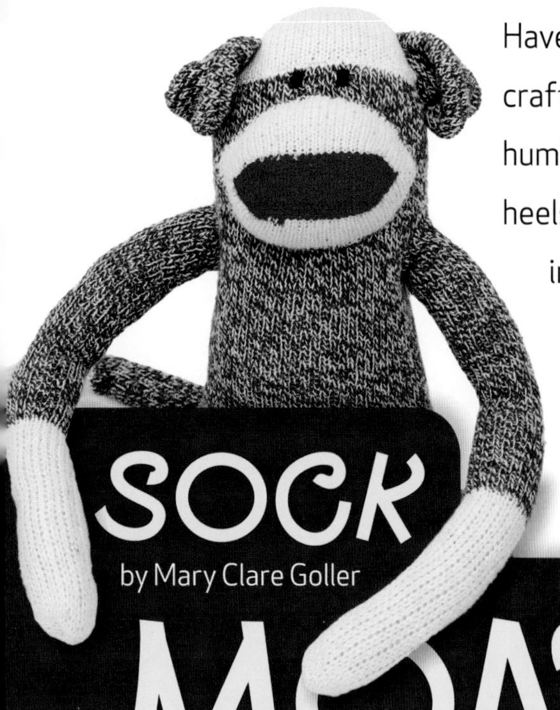

SOCK MONKEYS!

by Mary Clare Goller

Have you ever held a soft, cuddly sock monkey toy? This craft is an example of how creative people can **transform** humble materials to make something new. Socks with red heels were first knitted for factory workers and farmers in the late 1890s. It's hard to say who designed and made the first toy monkey using such socks. However, the tradition continues today. Follow these steps to cut, sew, and stuff a sock monkey that has a big personality and a lot of charm.

Step 1

Turn one sock inside out. Flatten the sock with the heel centered. You will make two lines of stitches that are about $\frac{1}{2}$ inch apart, as shown in the photo. When you finish each stitch at the sock band, make a knot.

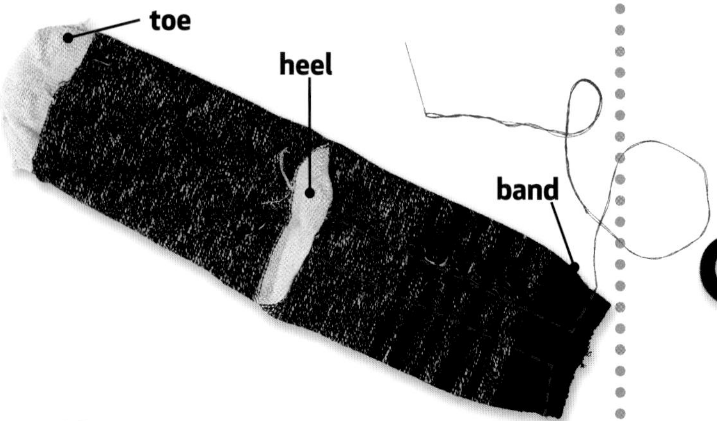

Step 2

Make a cut down the middle of the sock between the two lines of stitching. Leave an opening near the center of the heel.

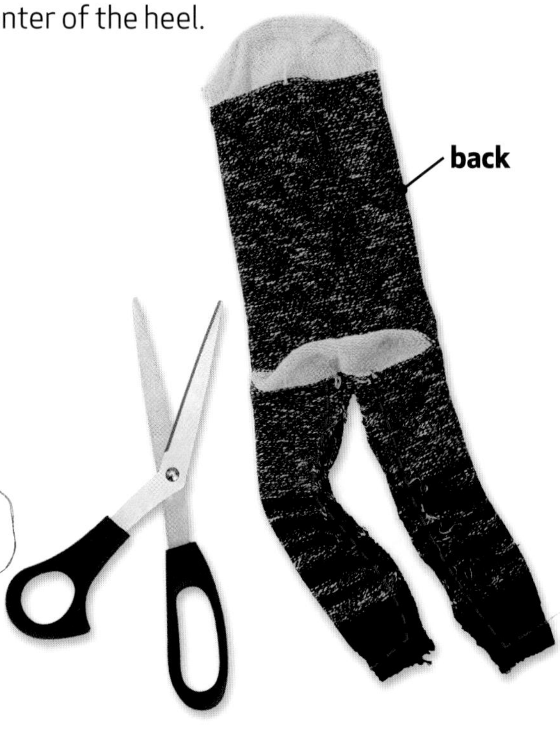

Materials

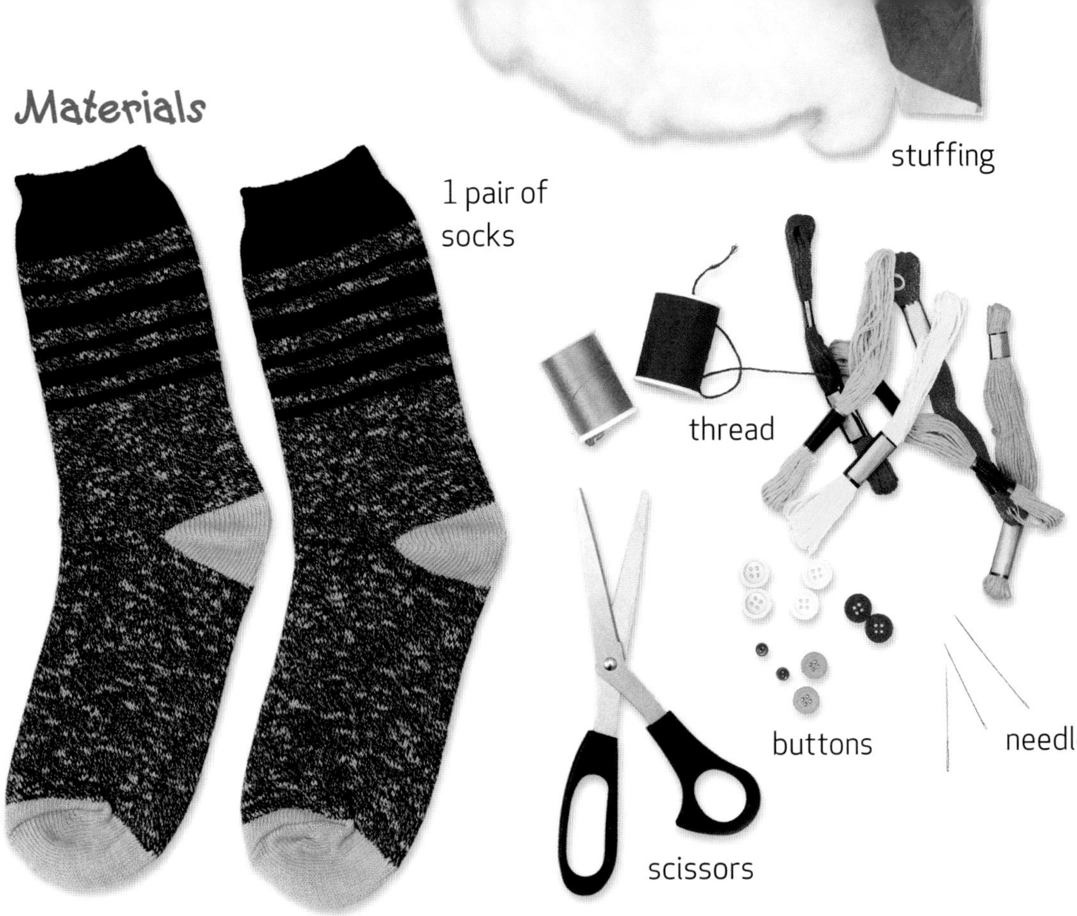

Step 3

Turn the sock right side out so the stitches are inside. Stuff the sock through the opening. You will stuff the monkey's legs and upper body.

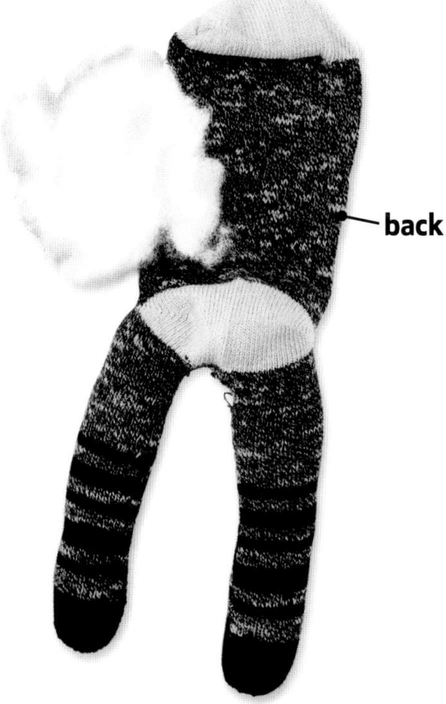

Step 4

Once the whole body is stuffed, sew the opening near the heel closed. You now have the monkey's body, including its head, without its mouth or ears.

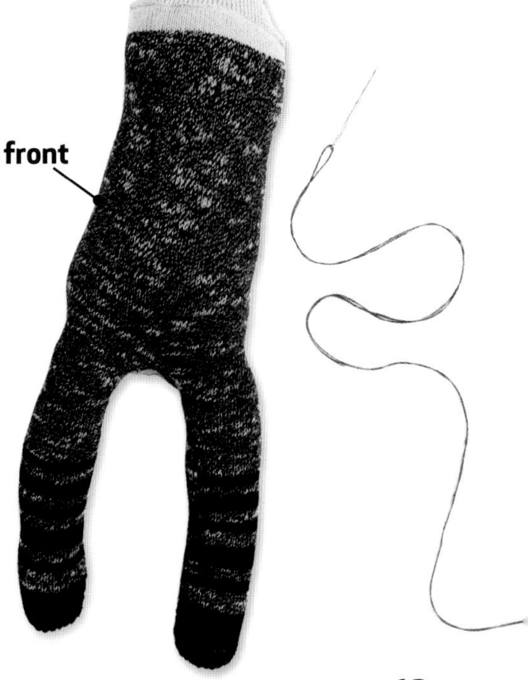

Step 5

Turn the second sock inside out. Cut the sock apart just above the heel. Make cuts to the bottom portion of the sock for the ears, mouth and tail. You will have one small, unused part of material.

Next take the portion for the arms and stitch two straight seams about $\frac{1}{2}$ inch apart. These stitches are like the ones you made in Step 1.

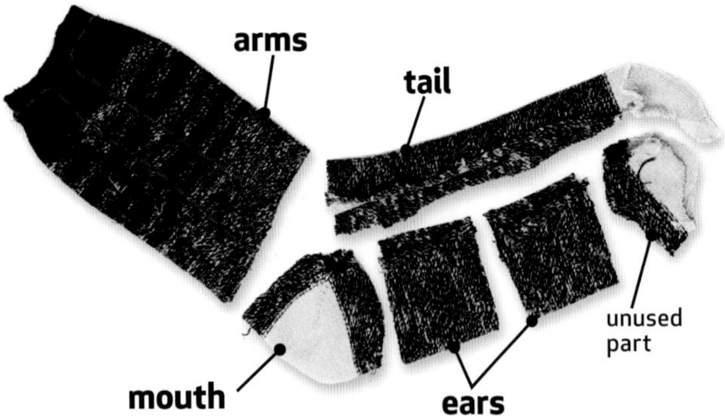

Step 6

Set the heel (mouth) aside for now. Sew a seam for the tail and stuff it. Stuff the arms. Sew around the edges of the material for each ear, leaving a small opening in order to turn ears right-side out.

Step 7

Attach the ears to the top of the toy. Close up any openings as you sew. Attach the arms and tail. Sew the body parts right to the body using small, tight stitches.

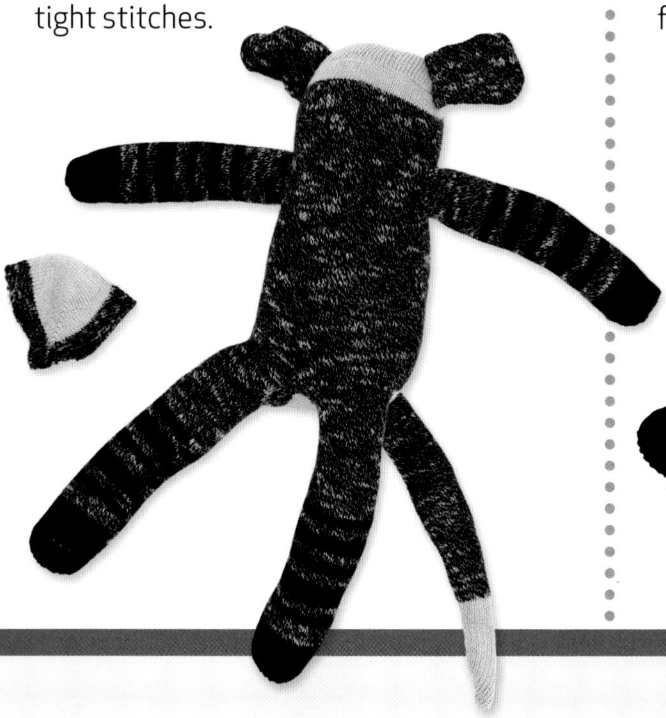

Step 8

Begin to attach the mouth to the face with small, tight stitches. Leave a small opening at one corner and stuff completely. Close the opening with a final stitch.

Finish your completely stuffed and sewn monkey with button eyes. Or sew soft eyes using only thread and stitches. (A monkey given to a baby or toddler should not have button eyes.) If you'd like, you can also add a stitch for a belly button!

Be proud of your **handiwork,** and keep practicing these steps with other pairs of **repurposed,** colorful socks, for a whole family of monkeys!

Check In What are the materials needed to make this toy?

GENRE Social Studies Article | **Read to find out** how two cities transformed unused places.

Urban Transformations

by Joseph Kowalski

Big cities mean a lot of people and a lot of buildings. In fact, the sheer number of buildings and concrete and metal structures seem to take up all the open spaces. When in use, these structures and the areas around them bustle with activity. But over time and for various reasons, people stop using the structures. When this happens, some structures may become **abandoned.** These empty and unused places seem to say, "Keep Out!" People steer clear until a day when someone looks up or around and can imagine the possibility of a **transformation.** This transformation might include ways to reuse, reinvent, restore, or **revitalize** abandoned structures and their surroundings.

From Highway to Urban Oasis

In the heart of Seoul, South Korea, an international city that boasts a population of more than ten million, a restored habitat and river runs gently through an area that once had a highway above it. An urban renewal project created a transformation, which redeveloped the unappealing highway area into a beautiful urban park. Ground level access to the once inaccessible Cheonggyecheon (Chung-gye-chun) River allows people to sit at the water's edge, ride along pathways, and enjoy a **repurposed** part of their city, long hidden away. Fish, birds, insects, and native plants have also returned to this restored habitat.

Partial structures of the old highway in Seoul stand in the river.

Before construction was completed, concrete structures blocked views of cityscapes in Seoul.

An aerial view during construction

Pedestrians can now walk across the river.

How did the transformation take place? The restoration began in 2002. It was completed two years and five months later. That is an amazingly fast time frame for a city development project like this one. Construction crews first needed to dismantle the elevated, concrete highway. Then all of the remaining structures, which blocked the stream, needed to be demolished. The project created thousands of tons of waste. But nearly all of the scrap iron or steel and concrete or asphalt was reused. Once the stream was open and flowing, the planners needed to consider the potential for flooding. Project developers didn't want to replace one problem—traffic congestion— with another—flooded streets. So the crews built embankments that will be able to withstand the summer rainy season and floods that come with the rains.

Planners also considered the aesthetic of the river, or the way it looks. Plantings give a sense of a natural landscape, far from the city. Some places along the stream are great places for people to relax, take their shoes off, and enjoy the cool water. The 5.84 kilometer (3.6 mile) river walk with a waterfall, brightly colored lights, and art installations cost the city billions to develop. So it was important to find ways for Seoul's citizens to easily visit the space. Planners included 17 access points from city streets above, which lead to the stream and walkway. The Cheonggyecheon restoration project reclaimed a natural resource of Seoul, its water. And it improved the environment and recreation options for its people. Sources have estimated that approximately 90,000 pedestrians visit the banks of this urban stream on an average day.

Seoul's urban river walk is edged with concrete. Yet it offers a natural habitat that citizens enjoy.

Old Line, New Life

Thirty feet in the air over bustling Manhattan streets in New York City sits the High Line. This rail line was once a track on which freight trains ran. It was in use from the 1930s until the 1980s. Then the rail line sat abandoned, a forgotten piece of history that became a blight residents had gotten used to ignoring. Many wondered if the city would ever tear down the unused structure.

For a couple neighborhood residents, this blot on the landscape sparked an idea. They wanted to reuse and transform what had become old and inactive. Two men initiated a project that changed an elevated eyesore into a sight for sore eyes. They helped create a new above-ground park, which now stretches across miles of city neighborhoods.

This plan for transformation was also an act of preservation. It would preserve local history and find a new use for the structure. "What a good idea!" others said. The streets are so crowded; it makes sense to have a park elevated above traffic congestion.

Reclaiming abandoned rail lines is a way to reuse existing structures in a city short on space. It also offers a safe and scenic passage through part of the city for New Yorkers and visitors alike.

An aerial view shows the abandoned rail line before reconstruction.

Weeds and grasses covered the old rails.

Landscape architects and gardeners maintain gardens along the sides of the walkway.

Sections along the walkway resemble railroad ties.

How was it done? After being neglected for 20 years, the High Line was already being reclaimed by nature. The old freighter train line was overgrown with wildflowers and weeds. The wild growth brought some inspiration. The Promenade Plantée in Paris, France was also an inspiration. It was created from abandoned rail lines, too. The neighborhood group, the Friends of the High Line, knew New York City would be a perfect place to try what Parisians had done.

Designers competed to earn the role of park planners. The winning team built the park to reflect the original character of the track. Features like the old railway ties were left intact. Native plants and grasses grow up out of the ties as they would in the natural world, only here they are carefully placed to create an artistic design.

The project is being completed in phases. It began in 2006 and development will continue. The High Line has quickly become one of New York's biggest new tourist attractions. Its beauty, combining nature with design, reflects the care and thoughtfulness of the project's planning.

In crowded cities across the globe, abandoned urban structures can become places to meet neighbors, enjoy the outdoors, and recall local history by enjoying a revitalized space.

Check In What remained the same and what changed in Seoul and New York City?

Discuss Information

1. What connections can you make among the three pieces in *Transformers*? How are the pieces related?

2. What does it mean to be a transformer? Use information from each selection to answer this question.

3. "The Quilters of Gee's Bend" and "Urban Transformations" tell about different types of problems and solutions related to transforming old into new. What are some of the problems and solutions?

4. What would you still like to know about the people or projects in Gee's Bend, Seoul, or New York City?